Southern
Messenger
Poets

DAVE SMITH, EDITOR

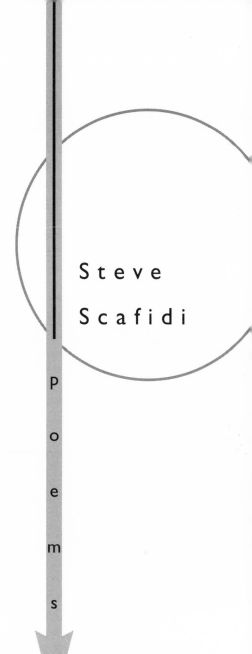

S t e v e

S c a f i d i

P
o
e
m
s

Sparks from a Nine-Pound Hammer

)|(Louisiana State University Press

Baton Rouge   2001

For my Family and for Kathleen,

who, like the pine trees

and the long hand of letters,

teach me to whisper, to lean

Manufactured in the United States of America
First printing
10 09 08 07 06 05 04 03 02 01
5   4   3   2   1

Designer: Melanie O'Quinn Samaha
Typeface: Sabon
Printer and binder: Thomson-Shore, Inc.

Library of Congress Cataloging-in-Publication Data

Scafidi, Steve.
    Sparks from a nine-pound hammer : poems / Steve Scafidi.
       p. cm. — (Southern messenger poets)
    ISBN 0-8071-2693-4 (alk.paper)—ISBN 0-8071-2694-2 (pbk. : alk. paper)
       I. Title. II. Series.

PS3569.C247 S63 2001
   811'.6—dc21

                                                                    00-051436

Grateful acknowledgment is made to the editors of the following publications, in which some of these
poems first appeared, sometimes in slightly different form: *American Poetry Review, New Virginia
Review, Shenandoah Southern Poetry Review, Southern Review, Virginia Quarterly Review.*
    Part of this book was written with the help of a grant from the Virginia Commission for the Arts.
    Great thanks to Sue, Leslie, Richie, Rick, Russ, Paul, Jan, Rob, Jack, Dave, and Norman.
    A special thanks to all my comrades at the shop.

The title for "Onlookers with the Burned Body of Jesse Washington, 18-Year-Old African American,
Waco, Texas, 1916" is taken verbatim from a caption in *Eyes of the Nation: A Visual History of the
United States,* Alan Brinkley, curator (Knopf, 1997).

Contents

Sparks from a Nine-Pound Hammer

Something New under the Sun

It would have to shine. And burn. And be
a sign of something infinite and turn things
and people nearby into their wilder selves
and be dangerous to the ordinary nature of
signs and glow like a tiny hole in space

to which a god presses his eye and stares.
Or her eye. Some divine impossible stretch
of the imagination where *you* and *I* are one.
It would have to be something Martin Buber
would say and, seeing it, point and rejoice.

It could be the mouth of a Coca-Cola bottle
or two snakes rolling down a mountain trail.
It would have to leap up out of the darkness
of a theater and sing the high silky operatic
note of someone in love. And run naked

slender fingers through the hair of a stranger,
or your mother or father, or grandfather, or
a grassy hill in West Virginia. It would live
on berries and moss like a deer and roam
the woods at night like the secret life of

the woods at night and when the sun rises you
could see it and think it is yours and that
would be enough and it would come to you
as these words have come to me—slowly,
tenderly, tangibly. Shy and meanderingly.

On the Occasion of an Argument beside the River Where I Live

Someone says we are trapped in language, and so the sun drops overhead
   through stilly pines where the river explains nothing and far away now
   several men and women on the Yangtze look up from their nets and
   point to the sky.
Bright Chinese fish, like all my words, struggle in the nets of a stranger.

But because there is no surprise nor delight in the hour of owl-call and
   locusts vibrating in the walnut trees, my friend despairs. All she hears
   are owls and locusts and though two grandfathers molder in the silk of
   their caskets and she loved them, the night is just the night.
And two men flying overhead from opposite directions embrace and hover
   over the house, kicking their long spindly legs. *Foolishness*, I hear one
   say, *foolishness*.

Tonight the chatter of things is enormous and also the silence that allows
   such chatter—the empty space the tongue clicks through to make a
   word, the cataract between atoms a light thing might leap.
So, if there is nothing here, then the absence of the river makes the river
   possible.

And the slow stripping of all my clothes makes the heat of this July night
   a bearable delight and a secret joy, walking down the driveway, to the
   bank of the river, over the water-worked stones, and into the current.
Laura, I don't know what you are doing but I am swimming naked in the
   Shenandoah and the sun is in China, still rising over the Yangtze.

And there is nothing for you here if two men can't fly skimming the
   surface of the water eating horseflies and laughing; and it is the truth,
   not my truth or some private certainty I tell you.
It is midnight and I sparkle like a trout.

Three Meditations on the Word *Night*

I

When the highest waving oak leaves
green and summery on the far trees
of the next ridge obscure the wide
round of the red sun and the Canada
geese holler briefly and the blue light
growing more blue over the Blue Ridge
mountains plunges suddenly into dark
officially the night has begun here
and meanwhile the western hemisphere
by degrees disappears from sight slowly
and to China the sun's high wheel
rolls and the poets there see it roll
over the prison yards and while my wife
boils pasta and I flick on the reading
lamp by the blue window of my room
someone hears the sound of his own
brittle white rib crack underneath
the strain of the speed of a fist
attached to an arm attached to
a guard attached to his government
furious to quiet the noise of words
that celebrate, simply, the mind's light
or lovers on the banks of the Yangtze
and when night falls in Shanghai
and the quick mopeds startle birds
leaping and diving over the city streets
looking for crumbs in the neon shine
of the evening coming on, it is morning
here and my father wakes and walks out
to his garden and bends quietly to the ground.

2

A period of darkness we may survive
or not as the earth moves around the sun
and this absence of any natural light
makes the cracking of a small oak twig
the footstep of something I imagine
with the talons of a large bird, the beak
of an owl and the arms of a man
from the Virginia State Penitentiary
and often at night I hear things
I can't explain and leave my book
and walk to the window to listen
dreaming the long stiff feathers
of its body and the orange beak
shining in the middle of its face
and it grabs me and the night forever
has been the domain of some worst fear
standing so outside windows planning
its way inside and a friend of mine
was raped for three hours one night
by a man who carried scissors through
her basement window and who said
ordinary terrible words very quietly
through his teeth as clouds passed one
after another lazily across the moon
hanging over her neighborhood that night
and why my feathery and malignant
imagination dreams of some nest
of branches and bones in the sycamores
outside my window and the razory
talons and the ripping, my friend knows.

3

While Romulus Augustulus in A.D. 476
around eight P.M. on a cool July evening
sighed under the weight of his queen
riding him gently like a horse crossing
the ruins of an empire, one barbarian
cooked a chicken on a small fire
in the center of the stadium under stars
glinting in that beginning way stars
glint dimly while the sky goes black
and the Dark Ages I always thought were
years of night unending in which no
light but torches or the slender blade
of the quarter moon helped the cobbler
in his shop drive nails into boots or
a man wash his face in a river never
knowing what he looked like and cities
for centuries functioned like early schools
for the blind and miraculous cathedrals
block by accurate giant block rose
to the moon and the illuminated books
of monks passed from hand to hand
like kaleidoscopes and wealthy kings
romped on the dark beaches of the lost
Mediterranean and often ships crashed
loudly and as people woke to the sound
gold fell through the pitch of the sharky
waters and the sudden depths were
as dark as the high crosses of the new
goliaths rising in the growing reaches
of the infinite black of the deep inky sky.

Sister Dream

Once when I was almost thirteen I walked in woods behind our house
and saw with the clarity of desire, and the need of puberty, a naked
lady with short furious wings rising out of a rocky pool as if to tell me
the secret of all secrets, her tiny breasts gleaming in the autumn light.

Once was the household spectacle of a man tying his tie. Once was
a woman bending to place a blue shirt in a blue basket in the house
where I grew up. Once was chimney smoke and a boy in love with
the sheer loneliness of walking for hours through woods in loneliness.

Now almost thirty and tired of secrets, puzzles, mirrors and the deep
mossy woods I have mapped for years on the backs of envelopes,
or stray sheets of paper, I see there is no intrinsic meaning to this
breathing in and out I pledged years ago to writing and finding out.

Once was a way to escape from death. Now only a low histrionic
comedic moan of *oh* when someone grows old enough to know
for certain he is living and dying. And no one on the earth can help
say what he has seen that rises naked and sad inside and gleams.

The Hayfield Chandelier

Two women comb their hair in separate rooms
of separate houses in the dark of a single night
on earth and one is my mother and the other
is her friend and this sentence is like a road
built for them to travel when they can or want

to travel out of loneliness at the end of the day
and meet and talk about whatever exactly it is
that my mother and her friend talk about now—
two figures in nightgowns in a hayfield sitting
at a table drinking coffee—and if you will, notice

how the bright September stars hang over them
swaying out like a chandelier and notice how
the road runs beside them like a kind of river
and the other few passengers of this sentence
do not disturb the peace but move on, quietly,

slowly, with their own business and some carry
yellow sacks on their backs and lean burdened
a little by their own moving and some will stop
to look up into the changing arms of maples
to see, maybe, the silhouette of an owl suddenly

leap silently in the night air but for the most part
the road is untraveled and the deep starlight
sways gently and casts just enough good light
for my mother and her friend to see each other
very clearly and a long time passes and laughter

carries to some of the houses along the road
and the laughter is rather loud someone thinks
closing his starry window and climbing back
to bed to sleep and the chairs in the hayfield
beside the road that my mother and her friend

lean back in as they talk are made of carved
Dominican mahogany and I don't know how
any of this ever happens—the language of long
friendship and the roads we travel at night, but
they do—these two. They are talking all night.

7

The Sublime

For Larry Levis

And what good is a dream finally? It breaks your head open
and cello music pours out of a stranger's window and the most
gorgeous woman you ever loved says to hit the road and you do
see them—that stranger and this woman. Kissing everywhere.

In the trees. On boats. In the kitchen cupboards. The fog
of daily life never lifts and the checkbook needs proper
calculations and the dog would like supper please and now
without warning the dream returns. It breaks your head open.

You lie there for a week and no one finds you until the dog
having lost its dignity finally eats and when there is no more
howls. It howls. And you are a missing person, a passage
of shit quivered into the dirt. A good boy. A terrible dream

someone picks up with a plastic bag wrapped in his hand
to throw away and you are thrown away. You do it every day.
Waking too early, driving to work, working and returning.
Reading poems of great beauty and crying at the movies.

Touching the hair of your niece who laughs at water. Flying
over cornfields so close and so openly that when you wake
there is silk in your beard. Your arms are tired and hang
at your sides like the wings of a migratory bird who is about

to die. And what good is a dream finally? It breaks your heart
and you stand in the lush dark of the moment after twilight
ends and begin to sing and nothing makes sense to you
and you sing louder for a while, then awkwardly sit down

where you are. And the stars overhead shine a little—no more
or less than usual—and whether it is daylight and they are invisible
or whether it is night and they are the embers of a blacksmith's
fire, they shine and you are grateful. That love is like a hammer.

Drinking Gift Whiskey

Between white miles of snowfall where the land drifts,
gliding black water sears the local cold hump of place
that is home to worn paths in briars and my father and I
who count, in the abacus of days, another dusk as the sun
disappears by degrees behind Shorthill Mountain.

We are working through January's arctic surprise
to cross, on foot, the unfrozen waters of the brook,
and step hand in hand as grown men in love from stone
to stone—a bottle of mash sloshing unopened, a gift
for a neighbor, in the wool pocket of the warm sweater
he wears, under his coat, to hold in what is precious.

And unforgivably lost here. Taking one false step
on a slick rock he takes us both into the cold Virginia
water he will die from in days. Alone, I am only writing
now to say we almost made it to the Christmas farm,
trees standing in snow like young scholars of the snow.

We almost joined them, slowly plodding across the field,
we almost made our way to the horse fence singing
its barbed melodies in the holiday wind. We, almost,
laughed our uncertain though light way into a neighbor's
coatroom fully drunk with journey's snowy work.

Now I return every cold day to stand on the misshapen
force-worn stones to feel the balance of who I am rock
back and forth in the wood's wind as bright precarious
birds make their familiar notes wing from oak to ash.
And I swear to remember this is the place of my beginning,

the one permanent moment where I learned loss is
lugging your body back to the house, breathing the air
of far pines on quick wind. Father, there are not many
words I know by heart as true as that late afternoon
when you began to die in earnest, but I have learned
for us, in the cold work of rescue that fails, some.

Lies

*I never knew him other than a man—with such staidness
of mind, lovely and familiar gravity, as carried grace
and reverence above greater years.*

—Fulke Greville

Sir Philip Sidney is balancing a wine glass on his codpiece
      while the ladies laugh and the wolfhounds sulk
           in the doorway. They want to leave the tower
   and the captive who has these women, he thinks, captive
with charm; a bell tolls, the glass drops and then the blushing.

Is it inadmissible to say that Sir Philip Sidney in all his years
      as a poet never once wore a codpiece or drank wine
           straight from the mouth of a seventeen-year-old
   duchess, who carried his daughter to term, then sold her
for the money to a man near Lancaster in the rain in 1576?

He invented gunpowder and carried a large printing press
      on his back. It shifted and itched. At night when
           the moon was London's only light he tore
   at the silk sleeves of his dressing gown and, bare-armed,
lumbered through the city whistling to the urchins and the cats.

He drank like Jack Kerouac! He shaved his legs once with a knife
      he found on a boat near Verona. Reader, he died
           with a sound in his lungs that went *ack,*
   ack, ack, a sword moving through his spine.
He wasted no time and loved the life of a man who lived to lie

in the third branch of the catalpa tree he dreamed up outside
      his yard which was basic in gravel and weeds. I am
           in love with what he saw once as a boy
   while riding a miniature pony on a road in the country:
day lilies alongside like rhymes to something cracked open wide.

The Pranks of Breath

For my father

You could set fire to a bag full of horseshit,
    knock on the neighbor's door and run away
to a suitable spot and watch the poor man
    stomp his feet to a fiery stink as you make
the one sound a child makes that isn't crying.
    His laughter sounds like a joyful dying.

You could throw walnuts on top of a tin roof
    where underneath a lady lives screaming
at you and your brothers who still can hear
    that thunder walnuts make and the other
summer thunder young boys break into.
    His laughter sounds like the moisture in a kazoo.

You could go to Catholic school and trick
    an old priest into thinking you are dying,
caterwauling on the classroom floor,
    lying very still until the place erupts with what
even the devil loves and honors and obeys.
    His laughter sounds like a flame's hurray.

You could tell involved spectacular lies
    to your children who believe and who race
out into the snow to find no man of snow
    on a horse of snow galloping wildly
through the snowy night though we listened.
    His laughter sounds like need's engine.

You could stand in the middle of the night
    in the middle of your house in the middle
of your life and tell yourself a long story
    that ends with sadness and silence, breathing
in sharply at what comes after. I know
    my father's laughter and love is what it's after.

Elegies

1 To the Fox Bill Shot

Night's leaping fire,
deep red diver lost
in the chicken wire,
I'm sorry you are shot.

And Bill's girlfriend's son
said he'd like the tail
and your tongue. Tiny
wild dog. Dead one.

You had to go hungry
to stay alive another day.
You didn't. Quiet now.
Pow. Quiet now.

2 To the Possum Bill Shot

Orphan one of ugliness,
sweet mother of Jesus
the dogs got and bullets.
Round gray monster of
my wandering and lost
wanderers, patron saint
of the quiet woods now

anarchic and pitch dark,
tonight I saw your mouth
unhinge in the death-yaw,
your tongue loll rolling,
your left back paw grip
air and now I sit here quiet
and write last words
to you—ugly other of
the lovely and the brutal
world I was born to too.
Go. I will follow you.

3 To the Beaver Bill Shot

A day after the night Bill shot you,
it's late winter and dogs carry you
to my house and not much is left
to hold in my arms, buck-toothed
madam of the birch and the saw,
sow of the moon, haunting rhyme
one teaspoon tells another quiet
in the kitchen light. I saw you,
closed my eyes and drank deep
from a cup the earth won't miss
the clay of. And this must be that
sorrow I've heard of and the day
we never dream of enough. How
sunny, unexpected and unloved.

4 To the Dog Bill Shot

I'm not sure what to say to you.
Days have passed.
I can't swim in the river
for seeing them dump you there.

Chicken-killer, stray shepherd
of the black and white
of days and nights. Goose-
killer, I can't swim in the river.

For hearing the shots. One, two.
For watching them carry you,
for watching the river—three,
four—all night tonight move.

On Looking into Golding's Ovid

It's still the same—he turns, she turns—the end
of a candle burns, maybe, in the eye socket
of a severed head. It's still the same wedding
guests who fill these straw canoes, who float
downriver swinging their lamps and calling
out for the groom. Orpheus is still mostly soil
splashing onto soil where the maenads squat.

Maybe a shepherd found a head and carved
the wet face from the white bone and now
dreams some strange version—a candle
glowing in his little room—of an early home.
It's still the same. Eurydice is cold or alone.
Or both. What if she ran ahead, long ago,
and overtook that man she loved, on the path.

What if she brushed quietly past him, and then
she looked back? I'm tired of stories of the asp,
and the wish of little wings where a god turns.
It's still the same. Every night, those revelers
calling from the water. I'd like to believe she
found a way out of the earth one night and then
reversed all that happened—I'd like to believe

she is wearing a wool shirt with tiny white buttons
along the arms, and that we have four children
who never visit and we eat long ornate meals
together in perfect happiness and everything
we ever wanted is ours for the asking and that
she would please quiet those strangers on the river.
It's still the same—he turns, she turns—story that burns.

Among the Millions of Things That History Will Forget

Orange zinnias growing wild at the blunt base of the Tower of Babel.
Bright blue glass and the blown-out footing of a Polish cathedral.
Three billy goats slaughtered by a farmer who is then slaughtered
by a drunk regiment of soldiers. The white bones of those soldiers.

The struggling body that is hanging from the rampart of a bridge.
My brother who loves the great failure of words to signify things.
Thomas, Thomas, Thomas, Thomas until sound unhinges and there
is nothing. You tell me history is just fragments, pieces and ruins.

You and I sitting together in a room of a house a hundred years old.
One whiskey bottle half-empty on the broad oak table between us.
The moted white-hot light of a reading lamp on your long black hair.
Quiet filling the house and Kathleen moving around some downstairs.

Whiffs of tobacco wafting faintly from where you pace all night.
My long sleep and the echoic narrative of dream's inordinate joy.
An old storybook read to children beginning *Once upon a time.* . . .
The ruins that become you. Ordinary things one devotes one's life to.

Ferocious Ode

It tells you the name of the flower you love.
It takes the shape of an old woman working
a pitchfork in the hay of a garden growing
voluptuously every day in your heart, that is

to say *it*, being mysterious, is difficult to
describe simply and with candor. It grabs
children in their dreams like tigers grab
gazelles. It grabs tigers. It makes me say

the sweet convolutions of poetry are not so
sweet sometimes and my grandfather claws
the red clay walls of hell for what he did to
my father. And I am happy on summer days

when the lily that I love bobs and sways
in wind like fire on a ladder. It matters.
Like a ladder on fire, it is spiritual. Like
the simile in which a house burns down

inside a boy, it is tragic. It turns and turns
laughing like a nun. It is nonsequential,
baffling and close to death like a woman
turning a pitchfork in her garden. Her diary

reads "I loved him." It is one page after
the last page in my grandmother's diary.
It is the afternoon and the sun is setting
coldly over my father's head—the oval

of which he has passed down to my sisters.
It is a family drama. It breaks dishes. It
runs to me with kisses, soft. And with claws.
It blooms at night also. My tiger lily. Loss.

Florence's Horse

For my mother

The house where she grew up is demolished.
A new family lives where she raised hers.
Long dead, the horse she climbed a tree
to reach and ride no longer runs and the tree
might yet or might not stand in upstate New York.

The thick blue coat of heavy wool she wore
in winter some other lady wears through snow.
The silk blouse of a pink so light it's almost
white probably flies through the dark air
in the form of swift high colonies of moths.

What's left of her passing over the earth is small
like a photograph and large like the house
where she stands in the photograph, one arm
around her youngest daughter: both looking
happily into this moment here, this one place.

Outside some children play in the sunlight.
It is a world despite the evils of our ending
century, a good place to live and grow old
looking into the future with your mother
or your daughter standing right beside you.

What we lose when we die must be what we
lose when we move from this breath to that,
from this house to that, from one locust branch
in upstate New York to the back of a horse
that is very fast. And beautiful, rushing past.

Twilight's Swimmer

Having jumped finally into the river and drunk it up,
his body floats for two days in May heat. Is found.
Claimed. Cleaned, but not displayed. Is imagined.
Now the sun rises over the resting ground and new
grass chirrs with the soft bodies of young crickets.

Someone says the syllables of the word *crepuscular*.
Someone else walks down a driveway to the mailbox,
laughs at a postcard. And the night comes. Question:
How many strangers are moving luxuriantly through
the velveteen privacy of their own separate inner lives?

On Tuesday, a man killed himself. He was a stranger
to me and though I live here on the river he leapt into,
no dead man reached into the sumac and tangled here
to cling loosely where I might find him. The paper says
little of who he was or why he wore the pants of a tuxedo.

He was bloated beyond his body's knowledge of limit
and was wearing just the yellow pants of a tuxedo.
That much I have heard. Question: Who among us
would not risk leaping into the unknown rush of a river
in spring to save a man? Who wears a yellow tuxedo?

Ghost. Brother. Stranger. Lost Soul of Someone Gone,
you died in the Shenandoah. Your body was found
about four miles north of here—a hideous muck of flesh,
mud and bone. I imagine you had black hair. I imagine
there is no end to weddings, strangers, and being alone.

The Twenty-Seventh Mile of a Marathon

For Lisa

The runner picks up speed and lifts off gently
from the blue slope of the earth's wide curve
and oceans pass beneath her: craggy shorelines,
the patchwork atlas of forest and field, the lush
dark of the world asleep. The runner dreams.

"Tell me," she says to stillness, "tell me a story
of speed and tell it to me fast for the light is
gaining and I will wake and with this body
break the barrier between what I dream
and what my dreaming means." My sister sleeps.

The runner lifts off gently from the blue slope
of the earth's curve, from the ordinary pacing
of her ordinary feet, and goes speeding through
the night as the world whirrs past—a blur
of trees, houses and streets. The runner dreams.

"Tell me," she says to speed, "tell me a story
of stillness and tell it to me slow for I don't have
far to go before this sleeping body's dreaming
stops and, having nowhere to go, this joyfulness
might also go, so tell it slow." My sister sleeps.

The runner speeds into the stillness of dream
and lifts off gently from the blue slope of earth's
wide curve, and what she knows of stillness
is what she knows of speed and all she knows
of dream is stillness and speed. The runner dreams.

The Sweet Life

After Heidegger

The house grows thirsty, walks
one night to the river and drinks.
A man thinks of god and sleeps.
Starlight crashes into the river.

What other language is necessary
to name the mystery of a night
in which a man thinks of god
as a house drinks from a river

lit with starlight? The living walk.
Ghosts walk. Even birds walk.
The word *walk* walks, tires
and sits on the edge of the river.

Old *climb* climbs the chimney
of the house beside the river
that flows, and sits like a bird
who watches the sky and sings.

Climb up and sing—god says.
Sing of divinity and the impossible
rapture of things. A man thinks
he is capable of anything before

he falls asleep and dreams. *God*
is a word I am capable of says
the night and *house* is a word
I am says the house as it walks

home slowly and gently wakes
the man inside who thinks this
life is a sweet life and language
says nothing at first, then laughs.

Winter Gossip

All the winter trees have roots so deep
they snag at the hats of the dead
as they pass one another on the dim
dirt streets and I'm told the city
there is like the burrow of a mole
but wider and steeper and the light
there glows like a white fat grub
grows for a season. I am told all
manner of bullshit concerning the dead.
Curled up in their cold beds, bulbs
of iris sleep shocked in the garden
with their white vegetable beards.
I'm told spring approaches but it snows.
Outside my window, black brittle arms
of a dying pine stagger through the air
like death's lost and drunken troupe
of puppeteers and I'm told to lighten
up. To buck up. To forget the gothic
fact living and breathing remind me
of every day a thousand times a day.
To watch fir trees move like young
women doing folk dances as the wind
makes a pattern of bright wild birds
on their skirts: sparrow, finch, sparrow.
Sparrow, finch, crow. I don't know
much of anything really to be honest.
I don't know what to trust of what I know.
I'm told spring approaches but it snows.
I'm told all of us go back so far in days
we are as ancient as the stars or older
and I imagine as best I can a place
billions of light-years long and see
the form of a woman lying in the shade
of a forest on heaven's rocky green
peninsula, and nude on the moss below
the spruce trees, beside that god of
my dreams, the devil lies and whispers
as he leans into the kiss and I guess just
before the creation of the world something
terrible, something wonderful, was going on.

To a Lady Reading

The whipsaw beloved noise of someone whispering
right in your ear. That and the sudden small
hillside of your left breast in your open hand.
A caress so tender it makes the earth break
under your feet. These sting the underneath
of my tongue and though they are only words
I love how they suggest a reality just outside
the separate ordinary saying of them. How shy
they appear exposed slowly on the page.
How you might watch them. How you
might actually pull your breasts out and over
the silk cups and let them hang there now
as you read, one hand holding my book.
That image took me a half hour to write.
This sentence especially moves tentatively
as a fingertip. And this one is even slower
lower softer and takes all day to go
this little way. If you want me to, I'll look.
Or else turn away quietly and tell you
how the night's fat pulley creaks
while the moon is hoisted up with rope.
How dreams turn. How want burns.
How tonight I just came up here and started
to write not knowing where it would lead.
Not knowing for sure if you ever reach late
in the day and touch yourself and rock
back a little in your chair and look out
the window while the Tree of Desire buds
blurry like a fire. Or ever think of me
pulling your dress up over your head slowly
from far away. From simple longing and sway.

The Facts of Springtime

The leafy ambrosial and half-midnight,
half-tender fact of simply thinking that
you might read this makes a pomegranate
of the moon and no one believes me or
even looks out the window to see if it's true
so used to metaphor and hyperbole's sweet
serpentine tongue that says everything
thrillingly and the fable and the desire
we are begins again as handsome Paris
must choose between three beautiful gods:
Athena who is wise, Aphrodite whose
tits gleam with sweat, and Hera whose
eyes are daggers and he thinks a minute
too long and chooses the wrong one and
suffers indignity and all that he loves dies
endlessly until his city is burned to cinder
and his children scatter hacked in the gore
on the ground where he kneels and he cries
as the pomegranate moon floats over low
battlements and thick red pools of hundreds
of gallons of ordinary human blood spill
in the clover of Troy's fields and rudimentary
streets and desire's meaning seems to be
tragedy's lure and it is, I am certain, mine
to follow as a swordfish doomed is dragged
by line much too fine to see and snagged,
hauled in, bludgeoned and eaten with
lemon tastes delicious to the devouring old
world we were born to endure somehow
still standing after all we have been through.

The Morality of Bodies

The stars were out and the moon was out glowing
the night Satan fell onto the earth with his oily coils,
the night Adam appeared from the muddy garden,
the night he dreamt of the companionship of a twin,
the night Eve looked at her hands and smiled,
the night the two discovered the difference between
the civilized and the wild, the hurtful and the good,
the secret and the discreet, the cock and the tongue
and the pussy and the one sweet thing in the world
without a proper name and from which came two
boys and then girls and towns and the rivalry
and the forgetfulness and the idea of relation
contracted to the immediate and wars broke
and the bodies lay there in the fields and mothers
cried out ripping their breasts and a sister held
her brother in her arms and a cloud formed over
a faraway city and millions of things were being
counted and billions and trillions and the stars
were out the night my friend lay in her life
as a girl in a gown in a bed in a town here
in America where her father still lives who walked in
to her room one night while the moon was out
and did to her what nations do to one another
also and when she told me I wanted to kill all
fathers and hold her in my arms not like a friend
but because she is, somehow, very directly
through the icy star-time of our suffering,
my sister and stronger than the night
someone wrote the first word in the first book
of the Old Testament carefully and cried.

Ode to And

Meanwhile the wracking minion of other lives carries on
violently and we don't exist a billion times you and I
forever and we never will and the girl with a scab forming
over her left eye looking at her hands and crying softly
in starkness Calcutta emerges from every day, cries on
and on until her head is in her hands and no one can help
not even her brother who finds her and holds her and not even
sudden beloved me who until this moment was as blank
to you as every other man and woman living an enchanted
daily number of years far enough away from yours to be
uncounted, unknown, and though your mother might miss you
one night and wear one of your blue shirts to bed in her
loneliness and your father look at the moon from death
you will remain anonymous and your grave's spring flowers
will bloom while your name eventually erases from the stone
and *and* the sweet ongoing little Jesus of words implies
we will meet in the starlit Hadean cave of nothing one
imagines the life after death must be—disbelieving rituals
April dreams of and it is a rare thing to say but everyone
I love still lives and soon the one by one of going away
grief is comes and I want whoever you are to somehow
enter my day with all the mysterious privacies and tender
joints and ankle bones and the lovely grace of that place
behind your knees no one thinks of and the soles of your feet
and to somehow talk a while so that when the last story your
grandfather told you lingers in the air between us and my wife
gets up from her creaking chair, the murderous ticking sticks
and is lost in the clock and the Shenandoah's new suicide
stops tangled in the outcrop of honeysuckle and her arms
motionless suddenly in the sway also motionless suddenly
hold something besides the wet sad fact of her death and while
you may not have known her name or wanted to hear
anything about her necessarily as often already we know
too much of one another, the newspaper says Judith Leslie
Hingis was born in Stafford County Virginia in 1956
in January and never says the texture of her hair was like
cornsilk when she was three or what creature appears
each night in someone's dream in another country far
away or why a train passes through my body and burning
meanwhile the stars tonight are turning. Or who you are.

This Page

If I only wrote about what I knew, as once
I was told to, this blank page would stand
forever as an example of honesty and candor.
A masterpiece of my reserve and silence.
Well, the conditional belongs to the dead.
My grandmother often said a tree grows
quietly in a meadow in the Old Country
in my head. My grandmother is sitting
with a book propped on her knees below
a sycamore tree in a field of harvested
soybean and the black birds fluttering
outside my window peck at the ground.
If only I weren't going to run outside
stomping my feet to chase them back
into the trees. If only they would turn
suddenly and fly towards me wildly
different with knowing that the fiction
we share—this mountain air, this life
we cling to—is only real in the sense
it is ours now, but no more beloved
than the other where my grandmother lies
on the ground looking at the sun through
the trellis of sycamore leaves coming in
this spring like dream's little sloops
on the bay of that place the dead go
when they come away from here, tired.
Restless. With a bag of oranges, a book.
A change of clothes. If only she would
turn to the page where I am writing this.
It's all I know—hello there—how to do.
Lonesome, Lonesome. And how are you?

Elegy for Emmett Till

The maple means to darken my house so slowly
and thoroughly that late winter's infinitesimal
first green bud whispers to its sisters and grows
buoyant in the running wind and I do not mind
the cruelties of April others despair of and longing
spreading in my chest as the hollowing darkness
of a tree spreads through the rings until it falls
and today I am thirty years old and want only
to live twenty more or so and the men I work with
every day, attending to the broken elegance of antique
chairs and mirrors the wealthy abuse, worry some
when I cry out blasphemies and prance around
the shop as if the lightning bolt intended quietly
for my poor head would miss and deprive their new
children of good love and money, and these men
I love who grow soft bellies and gardens patiently,
endure the sun and the moon and the scorchings
of blood breath sends through their hearts so fragile
paper is torn with less force than at times they
will turn away from some dumb thing I've said and
since every day the world wills we stay this far
from death we are a kind of testament of luck
I apologize for my ugliness and to the woman once
who sucked my cock and whose name I cannot say
for hurting her again I apologize and really there is
no end when you think of the easy stupidities of
your life which actually seriously ends and even now
every man and woman has some shimmering future
anecdote of tragedy another will pass on sad maybe
telling the news of my cancer or the cars crashing
that strangers, who had names and no idea that today
was the day, drove and the unrelinquishing wish
the body has for life never-ending extinguishes
and what's next glories in the high likkered-up
rhetoric of those left behind and so the beauty
of the rose with its sexual concentricities of soft
flesh and delicateness sways through a thousand
years of human passage as an image to replace red
actual goop blooming under the skull of someone

whose life was taken away and broken over
his body and I think of Emmett Till's grandmother
the moment she heard the news of his lynching
and how she flew from the grave and held his lost
bewildered shade under the shade of a beautiful
child's wrecked body and the things that she said
to comfort him are the secrets, I suspect, we will learn
when death's mob swarms and cusses and drags
us away and the great ignorance of a great many
white southern men is no secret at all anymore
and so this afternoon in the tunneling raw flume
of honeysuckle too wintered to burn green I saw
a rabbit who saw me first and its left eye got
very wide as the twittering swift things in the trees
moved and the wild awe that this day began once
some millennial tick ago, in the somewhere physicists
think of, will never end though we pass through loudly
making breathing sounds or skyscrapers or wheels
for dreams we jack up and joyride screaming
in all night in the mysterious way some nights my wife
will and not remember and when the day comes
and the maple's canopy wrecks the sun's interminable
looking with its sea of shades of the deepest green
I will know it is summer and walk to the river
and swim while nothing grabs at me whispering.

For the Last American Buffalo

After a photograph by Richard Sherman

Because words dazzle in the dizzy light of things
and the soul is like an animal—hunted and slow—
this buffalo walks through me every night as if I was
some kind of prairie and hunkers against the cold dark,
snorting under the stars while the fog of its breathing
rises in the air, and it is the loneliest feeling I know
to approach it slowly with my hand outstretched
to tenderly touch the heavy skull furred and rough
and stroke that place huge between its ears where
what I think and what it thinks are one singing thing
so quiet that, when I wake, I seldom remember
walking beside it and whispering in its ear quietly
passing the miles, the two of us, as if Cheyenne or
the lights of San Francisco were our unlikely destination
and sometimes trains pass us and no one leans out hard
in the dark aiming to end us and so we continue on
somehow and today while the seismic quietness of
the earth spun beneath my feet and while the world
I guess carried on, that lumbering thing moved heavy
thick and dark through the dreams I believe we keep
having whether we sleep or not and when you see it
again say *I'm sorry* for things you didn't do and
then offer it some sweet-grass and tell it stories
you remember from the star-chamber of the womb
or at least the latest joke, something good to keep it
company as otherwise it doesn't know you are here
for love, and like the world tonight, doesn't really
care whether we live or die. Tell it you do and why.

When This Book Comes Out I Am a Dead Man

So many thousands just like me full of good intentions
sit down now to write all of us together by a spidered
window cracked, by the Great Pyramids, by a man
eating peanuts on a Greyhound bus looking over at us
occasionally to smile wondering what we are doing and
often I think it is nothing and dusk falls like a curtain and
often it is nothing and saying so makes the curtain rise,
the peanut-man look into the desolate lights of Baltimore
and the sun a familiar presence behind the eyes of a woman
blind since birth looking out her window in a Cairo slum to
my window and whoever the others are and some I know
and some I love must carry on without me now—good-bye—
and often these evenings in May when Kathleen goes to sleep
the moon's behind the mountain and the firelight of something
green kindles in the leaves around the house and a figure like
Death in Bergman's *Seventh Seal* but bonier, quieter flies,
robes flapping in the wind of his descent, and circles overtop
the house like some vulture-king of my imagination merely
to sit on the lowest branch of the pine tree and look at me
I swear to God all night and once I wrote on an envelope
thirteen times for luck the terribly embarrassing sentence
I will write poems of great beauty and power, and though
Death thinks this is funny and some of my friends also laugh
right in my face, it is true my mother's body grinds quietly
into the cold ground and my father already walks on his knees
and you perhaps have seen, as I have not, the sudden shock
of light on the blocks of the tomb of Cheops or heard a rhyme
suck half of Manhattan into its open hatch as if it were
that UFO in all the movies this summer and "It can't happen
to me, it can't happen," Death says pointing, mocking me,
and if that old So-and-So who made the first white light
of the first day of the rest of our lives comes down to me
outright as he did to Moses somewhat burning as he spoke
I'd lower my voice to a silence even bees cannot hear
or dust mites or atoms furiously listening in the spinning
air and ask what kind of fool are you to make me want
anything of great beauty and power when all I can do is
think of death and so many like me full of good intentions,
you fucker, I hope you burn in the hell you have invented for

people like me and that you forgive me as I have forgiven
you not at all for making what from you is never taken
and never was despite the words I love: *light, loss, was.*

Who Wants to Know What Love Is Worth?

All my friends abandon me to work and the joy of their own lives
and name their babies after myrtle trees and the dead. And so
to hell with the objective and the correlative. I am sad and blame
everyone on this earth for sadness. And so to hell with the dark

capabilities of birds. Let the sad catastrophe of breath begin
its lame circulation through my lungs and let this dream of life
after death make its course in a blue journal few will read.
I do not care who knows my secrets and don't want yours.

The wisdom we glean is small change. Who wants to know
what love is worth is a sucker. The force of two bright wings
on the smallest bird imagined haunts who imagines and the engine
is small like the kind on a chainsaw. Two cycles. And all I want

from life is to turn and turn and fall once again deeply in love
with love and be delusional to the point almost exactly
of incarceration. To say *It is spring* and stall Time long enough
to watch my lover undress and to oink like a pig at slaughter

when she comes to bless my body with hers. When she says *Oh,
yes.* It is spring, John Keats, and you are dead and I am sorry.
Truth and beauty are not all I need to know. They never were.
Though important, I need something more. It hums and whirs.

To Publius Ovidius Naso

Backwards I have read your book and seen the river-
leaping-head of Orpheus return to the wrecked body
that weeps and turns and walks in hell and sings
on his wedding day and the happy life he led before
he loved her and they never met and the narcissus

flower turns to a drowning boy and the boy an egg
in his mother's body and she also returns growing
tiny now and I love how the earth in the end is
nothing at all and backwards I can see always
what I am and everyone alive now zeros to a cell,

and so on until Eden's shimmering sapling's green
appearance precedes the dark and in that dark
before starlight and gods, all of who we are is
present it seems as promise and swirl and the wind
rising now out my window is cousin to the quick

first breath of that thing I can't imagine whatsoever
that preceded all preceding and lurks still in the trees
like a black snake or a man with wings malevolent,
dire as Gabriel, and the forward billion of our years,
some of which you lived in singing, I stand in now

wondering what Rome smelled like after a sudden
rain when trees budded like nipples and you walked
home from Corinna's house—your sex still humid,
your left arm's bite-mark beading a little blood, Ovid,
I wonder what thought crossed the membrane of your

knowing just before death and on your way to death
so fast that a last thought meant nothing perhaps since
you couldn't sing its meters softly to a naked woman
and today in April I swam nude in a mountain creek
so cold my teeth still vibrate and I thought you might

want to hear how the sunlight shattered on the water
and how desire for a woman still makes a man go
write his poems in the middle of the night when the rain
smell of love is the smell of Rome and how my wife
sometimes moans. How I shall be living always also.

The Bee of Was

The angel in the wheel and the forest in the man
and the old in the cold, cold bottomless Real
turn the world we don't understand and turn
dirt to roses and the tiny hands of the dead
grip the levers and the handles of the machine
that lifts the lifted moon from the wide blue sea
that says "Enough, enough, it's never enough,"
this chuff-chuff of want being is the gerund of,
and if you have the money you can go to the fair
and if you love a man, or if you love a woman,
or sing the name of my Aunt Rachel's husband
you can see the dazzling lights of the city of Jack
from the billboards and parlors and Christmas lights
to the smokestacks smoking and the Ferris wheel
rolling toward the bay and the pleasure boats of Be
you are the captain of, and *see* say sailors pointing
at the moon and we go where we want to—wild
little bee of the common and the grave, the common
grave where some still lie terrified and alive who,
while the backhoe moves and the wives of killers
cry in rooms, begin to move a little, long dead now
to dying and the keyhole light of another day, saying
"I remember breath and the one word breathing said
was *yes*," and I remember when love was a dress blue
and breasts and I remembered you a long time after
you took yourself away and left and I remember
my mother's hair and my sister's hair and the nonsense
of the spoon and the loneliness of the happiness of
the long and the cold and the wheel and the song
here in the forests of the deep of the afternoon.

The Latitudes of Desire

She walks into the room wearing only her blue panties
and I love how the word *panties* ends on a teasing
slide as if the sheer glide of the silk were now
between my teeth and the sounds of *knees* and *please*
relieve the quick pant and lace of her walking in
almost completely naked as I lie very completely naked
on the bed and watch as she walks into the room with
only her blue panties between her and me and the world
drinks a Coke while she walks the thin line of the 39th parallel
that runs through our bedroom like a tightrope and extends
eastward as she takes the long way to my waiting arms
through Baltimore where Edgar Poe broke a rib trying
to suck his own cock on a sunny late April afternoon,
and she walks across the Atlantic in her blue silk panties
and the water heaves and rises and wets her feet a little
as the walking days pass like frigates and barges
loaded with bananas, and she strolls through the Azores
tickling the mustache of a stranger with her fingertip
and in Lisbon her breasts red from the voyaging sun
inspire young painters who hunger suddenly for the rich
seedy meats of fresh tomatoes and she walks toward me
the long way, in her blue panties, like the Aphroditic dream
I have married and oh the walk is long and she walks
across ferry-boats of the Mediterranean in her blue panties
and her gold hair shines as she crosses the moonscapes
of central Turkey where no one lives and talks to the goats
bearded and horned as I am by now and the goats look
up at her as she moves through northern Iran and maybe
one eye of one goat watches her disappear over
the horizon and it takes forever as her blue panties
still cling to her hips and the taut lines of the silk
stretch and move as she walks beside the fishermen
reaching out to her and touching their cocks as they fish
the Caspian and bob in their boats and the bed rocks
slightly and adrift I watch her step into the sudden heat
of Samarkand's late-evening streets full of baskets,
merchants and children racing by as her blue panties
shine in the sun and this can't last too much longer I tell
her while she moves patiently, quietly through all

of China crossing the wall, clambering easily graceful
through the prairie grass emperors filled their mattresses
with and would now trade everything they once had
to merely graze her blue panties and her ass with their
hands but she is coming my way through Pyongyang now
her arms working slowly relaxed by her side, her belly
full of the kind of bright butterflies mine is and which
fly round her head in northern Japan where this butterfly
is exclusive, exquisite, and one lands on her eyelash
as she heads into the great blue Pacific Ocean whose salt
I can smell already impatient to pull her blue panties
down and my body can't wait any longer but waits
in a kind of tremble as she re-enters America through
the clean streets of Sacramento where all the jugglers drop
their chainsaws, their apples, and watch as I watch
this beautiful woman pinch her nipples occasionally,
slowly, or run one finger in the slowest stroke of luck
Nevada never dreamed of as she moves closer to me
and her blue panties are like the sky about to fall
as she goes right over Pikes Peak and waves
to me and I can feel her breath on my neck as Kansas
City suffers the warmest breeze it ever knew
and men nearly come on the street as she passes
walking home to me these few thousand steps across
the prairies and the rivers of our room this evening
in April in the Blue Ridge Mountains wildly in bloom
with bluebells, violets and irises, all of which now
glow somewhere in the world like Kathleen's silk panties
lying on the floor in the dark, lying there in the dark.

Naked Sunlit Afternoon with Vultures

The charismatic bodies of the dead draw them down
quietly imperceptible from the circle in the sky
to the sycamore trees and the roadside we see
every day decked in the common gore our speed
leaves behind for these birds to pick at slowly
who strut and stutter primitive things hungry
to eat and be glutted by death. O Byzantine
black angels always smelling at the aftermath
of a sad fact, today in the very middle of one
beautiful afternoon you watched me strip down
to boots and wander a deep creek's boulders—
water falling everywhere—and in the blue sky
descended to the near trees as I splashed, sank,
swam and then spread out on a rock with lichens
stuck to my body, as one by one you passed
exactly between me and the sun so your shadows
touched my body quickly as I guess you looked
for some living reflex or reaction and did so then
receive one as I waved and called you all near
wondering if perhaps one brave starved member
of your community too zonked on sunlight to wait
for my death would come at me and the idea
of wrestling you to the ground and breaking you
apart in my arms was wonderful as meanwhile all
eight of you settled in the near trees scritching
anxious in the branches while I breathed the air
my winter body shared with your dark wings
and so on this beautiful day too full of the sun's
bright clarity and the joy of swimming naked
and too full of late April's mosses and buds
bursting on the muscle trees, your eerie hard
leering was part of the promise I have made to
Kathleen and my family and the dearly beloved
friends I live to delight here in these long letters
to never kill myself or anyone else or thing now
moving quiet suddenly under love's low wheel.

The Mower and the Moon

Black heavy puffings of smoke suddenly under
the peach tree and the summer quiet sudden
also as the engine cuts and the waft and green
loft of mown grass and the dizziness of sun
and the burn on the back of my neck all amount
to some new kind of attention as I wheel slowly
this heavy thing into the stillness of the cool shade,
tip it over and feel underneath its carriage
for the nubbin of bolts and loosen them counter
clockwise and take off the blades, sharpen
them in the spark-light of my neighbor's garage
where the grinder spins, and then I must change
the oil and the dark pearly stream flows down
and the amber new oil goes in while two
rabbits huff in the tall grass nibbling a thing
or two I have grown in my garden—lettuce
like the private foldings of silk, a radish
like a nipple, and the mower is ready again
and I pull the lovely string and pull it
again and again until something small fires
and the world responds and how often I have
spent warm afternoons walking behind this
whirring thing is a magic number like the one
corresponding to the stitches in the silk blouse
blue and shiny hanging there on the clothesline
corresponding itself to the horizontal form
of the woman sleeping on the sofa in the dark
of the living room corresponding to the bright
hills of the moon, the sun overhead heaving
slightly westward as she dreams we're nude
upstairs moving slowly trembling as I mow.

Icarus on the Beach in the Afternoon

Revived by the cool water and the plunge and breathless,
Icarus swam back to shore, toweled off and told the world
the news of his demise was premature and shouted
his name to the sun and millenniums passed, rockets
touched the moon and crows this afternoon fly calling
in gangs as the dead men and women of the earth
remain in their elementary parts and spin atomic still,
still here, while the black antenna of an ant tall
in the palm of Kathleen's hand sways to her breath
and shivers and what vibrant dream the ant has
the ant is, moving now as the month of June
passes and no one will die for a second here
and no one will be born and a man will fly
hovering low over a beach and scream with delight
in his nakedness and lift up toward the sun quick
and up and up until he is a dot and the world
goes back to its business and a lady clutches
her chest and falls to her knees and a young father
newly made weeps somewhere and the generic white
pills of the stars appear and the Minotaur defecates
in the catacomb and reads a letter he has found
in the modern factory-stitched pockets of his
victim's shirt and there is word of love between
a man and a woman, of how she cut her father's
hair one afternoon under a maple tree, of how sad
she has been and of the labyrinthine green of young
nasturtiums and when the monster sleeps he dreams
of her and today in the United States of America
it is almost summer and whatever breaks now
inside you remains so and Icarus on that day
walked back home and drank and learned one
or two trades to get by as his descendants here
in Virginia have done and while it is easy
to go on talking with your wife or kissing her
shoulder it is harder to stop what you are doing
now and look at the sun and make your own new
important designs and you were asked to perhaps
begged to, born to, in some way lift up right now
the whole of yourself and fly as in dream through

the streets of the sun and travel back and forth
between the world you know and the other,
whatever it is, one you have heard of, just as now
you travel between the word *love* and the thing
burning up and back again. You. O survivor.
Wax-wing, flyer, reader, writer. Citizen of desire.

To a Lady Still Reading

1

There is a man who wants to—
with the light willing zillion
nerves of his left hand's good
fingertips—graze the small slope
of your left tit so slowly, so
softly, that it's small succulent
companion tenses also rising up
just a little in the slow way
our bodies in increments heave
under our clothes and he wants to
unbutton a button in the middle
of your shirt like a magician
slipping his hand in looking you
in the eyes as the risen hard
surprise of his being here beside
you rises and why not sway there
a moment. Now. Go find him.

2

A ballet slipper. John Updike said
the tantalizing fit of the inside
of a woman when your cock
enters and her warmth surrounds
yours perfectly is a kind of rightness
that has no match though a dancer
before the dance slips on her shoe
as the foot disappears smoothly
slowly into the darkness and what
follows is accompanied by music
and the muscled hot moving of
bodies and so a man who loves you
always with the calm of a dancer
now wants to dance with you—
to feel the prickly dark curls,
the nubbin and the tender supple
warmth of grace. Now. Find him.

I Won't Go Lying Down

Unready, unready, how unready I am—
and we go—hard and fast hovering
with a mind of sleigh bells or snow
over the horizon—o—we go friends
nowhere we want going to the usual
death and circumstances so please
no more complaining of loss in magic
languages and hurt come to crack
your back and laugh—let's just go
quietly for once as we were asked
long ago perhaps—to Timbuktu,
to the shiny white beach of breath,
to who, you know, calls to you.
Your wife will wait. Your career.
Your children. The moon and sun.
And unready, how unready we are.
Even the suicide says so closing her
eyes while the bullet flies through
the tissue and the silicate bone
and you are alone even now lost
with me floating out here quietly
in the uneasy open and kidding
ourselves I hope is some sacred
activity to be counted in our favor
when the crappy whole of our loved
days is measured and filed away
and unready, how unready also
Death will be when we arrive—
still tucked in his little brass bed.
O sleepy Angel Death, wretched
clerk of the blessed earth, I hope
you have eyes in the back of your head.

The Mission Chairs

For Nick Greer

They are seated in plain sturdy chairs
from another century and fly right over
your house and mine and the dark fields
in between where cattle sleep, and over
the leaning white barns of Lovettsville,
and over the gardens of New York City
and over the Lake of Great Monsters
where things we have never seen roam
the bottom rocks of granite with grace.

Over the hovels of India and the slender
deer paths of a deep wood, they go
flying over the Ganges, that holy river
of skulls and jewels, and they go flying
over the Himalayas with great ease
waving to the nomads and the sheep
and they fly through the snowy streets
of a city in the Ukraine where a boy
crashes his gold bicycle into a shed.

And they fly over the whole miraculous
earth shaking their many bony fists
at the passengers of airplanes who
quietly piss themselves, and they fly
alongside pelicans who fly along
the rocky coastline of south China or
Half-Moon Bay where abalones lock
themselves inside themselves with
all their delicious and difficult muscle.

And sometimes, in their straight chairs,
our lost beloved dead fly down low
and harass commuters of large cities
by landing their heavy souls on top
of the shiny roofs of slow-moving
cars and maybe it is your grandfather
seated in his antique chair, reading
Tolstoy to Tolstoy, cruising down
Lexington Ave. on top of a limousine!

For I have seen such a thing in words
and it is good to be able to tell you
one of the few secrets I have learned
from spying, and though I do not know
why the dead are flying around or why
they insist on sitting down, I do know
they leave the cold ground and the fact
of their passing over the house tonight
is the old oak and slat-back fact of hope.

True Stories of Bullets

For Vedrain Smailovic

1

It was a November afternoon in Lucketts
Virginia a couple of years ago and hunting
for deer along the Potomac River a man
sitting on the ramshackle pine boards
nailed in the crook of a poplar tree
saw, aimed and shot a young doe
through the gut and the huffing noise
was startling it was so loud it was
he said like the sneeze of something
otherworldly and the deer took off fast
wheezing and listing through autumn
bluffs of honeysuckle and crashed away
as the man climbed down clumsy
from the tree and cut his right arm
open above the elbow and took off
after the deer watching the red trace
of gore on the leaves and when he saw
the quarry there suddenly facing away
and leaning into the river for a drink
as it died, this man dropped his gun
and ran leaping to tackle the thing
and jumped up onto its back reaching
forward and so plunged into the river
wrestling and snapped its neck finally
and when he drug it from the water
he searched and found no bullethole
in this deer and lay there exhausted.

2

And the world—I am told—it moves
so that constellations with Chinese
names and Chinese purposes hover
exactly over my house as it moves
under the Chinese sky and the Chinese
afternoon is a beautiful evening
in Virginia and I point at the moon
and revolve with everyone else
like the earth is some gigantic ride
and the Malaysian sky passes over,

the Honduran sun passes over,
the Norwegian and Zulu moons,
the Navaho noon, the Antarctic
stars all hover and pass over me
standing in my yard now pointing
as the oldest root of the word *story*
means "to see" and I'll tell you this
once when I was eighteen traveling
through Yugoslavia on a dark train
in the stupor of being young and home
sick I stuck my head out the moving
window and looked at the moon
that was a round red wobbling
sphere and was happy to see
something so beautiful it was like
the lost summer night of a boy
once in Virginia shooting the moon
with a small .22 and watching
it fall slowly into the quiet woods.
The next night there it was. Like new.

3

While a shell fired and rose higher
over a city under siege and the rumor
of bread led scores of citizens out
into the streets and one bakery sold
bread to the gathering line and death
arced over the steeples of churches
and plunged into the crowd blowing
into the ears of many who fell a man
nearby went crazy finally deciding
to wear his tuxedo again and to play
the Hadean bellows of Albinoni's Adagio
on his cello at four P.M. every day
for twenty-two afternoons in honor
of the number and the time these people
he loved died in their own quick
lost blood that spattered and ran

on the stones that day on May 27
1992 and Mr. Vedrain Smailovic
walked through Sarajevo to this place
with his chair and his instrument
on the days afterward and the music
he sawed defiantly with his bow
across the strings rose up willowy
among the snipers' miscalculations
and the bullets were a part of what
he played and the twenty-two muddy
graves and the gentlemen in the hills
firing away and the sun's bright
mesmerism and he leaned so hard
into the sound he made, it moaned.

4

Still going that other deer ran crooked
I imagine banging through the woods
bleeding to death and didn't get far
before lying down in autumn cold
and the frost and it must have been
sassafras, oak, sorghum and grass,
the blur of things familiar the deer saw
pass as it ran through the woods and
the world went by rolling underneath
the deer who seemed to move and did
run hard and yet stood still and quiet
while the ground rolled and the deer
pushed the earth is how I see it—pushed
with its hooves and stayed in place
while we moved—you and I and all
the bright cities and the dark cities
passing in tandem under the sun then
the moon and the sun again as we
I don't think will live to see the day
this deer really dies, my metaphysical
dying doe, my new theory as we
go to death and every story I love

goes there like a pilgrim and what
we will find there is anyone's guess
and mine is a six-pack of Pabst
and a long conversation with god
about the past and kissing the hand
of Frank O'Hara and the eyelashes
of Marilyn Monroe and calling out
hello to the dying moving the world below.

For the Eighth Annual Celebration of St. Cecilia, the Patron Saint of Music, Purcellville, Virginia, November 1999

In the golden spruce front of a violin,
     there in the alternating lines of dark and light
         like sometimes the rain or
     rays of the sun fall down, you can see
as you can hear all you ever knew once shimmer

and disappear as the violinist plays and what
     he plays is all you know and all you have
         for the long little while
     he plays and he plays so magnificently
the men and women in the crowd beside you

disappear with you by astonishingly sweet degrees
     and the years pass and your best suit crumbles,
         your teeth plink to the floor
     as timber by timber the roof caves in,
snow blows through and centuries later wolf packs roam

the wreckage of folding chairs and carry your white bones
     to the new hills of ice growing outside
         what was once Purcellville
     Virginia and when I think of music
so great no passage of time could ever kill it

I think of some future day far away I hope
     when a mouse pulls some brown grass through the hole
         it gnawed in the very
     last violin lying somewhere half smashed
in the charred ruins of the shiny ancient cities of

Cleveland or Sacramento and when I think of
     that future day far away I hope
         I think of the golden
     spruce face of a violin being
played well right now somewhere on the planet

maybe on a mountain in Colorado or a concert hall
     in Havana or along the coast of Nigeria
         in a fishing boat
     or here where I listen now for the cello
joining in and the flute joining in with the violin.

To Whoever Set My Truck on Fire

But let us be friends awhile and understand our differences
are small and that they float like dust in sunny rooms
and let us settle into the good work of being strangers
simply who have something to say in the middle of the night
for you have said something that interests me—something of flames,

footsteps and the hard heavy charge of an engine gunning away
into the June cool of four in the morning here in West Virginia
where last night I woke to the sound of a door slamming,
five or six fading footsteps, and through the window saw
my impossible truck bright orange like a maverick sun and

ran—I did—panicked in my underwear bobbling the dumb
extinguisher too complex it seemed for putting out fires
and so grabbed a skillet and jumped about like one
needing to piss while the faucet like honey issued its slow
sweet water and you I noticed then were watching

from your idling car far enough away I could not make
your plate number but you could see me—half naked
figuring out the puzzle of a fire thirty seconds from
a dream never to be remembered while the local chaos
of a growing fire crackled through the books and boots

burning in my truck, you bastard, you watched as I sprayed
finally the flames with a gardenhose under the moon
and yes I cut what was surely a ridiculous figure there
and worsened it later that morning after the bored police
drove home lazily and I stalked the road in front of my house

with an ax in my hand and walked into the road after
every car to memorize the plates of who might have done this:
LB 7329, NT 7663, and you may have passed by—
I don't know—you may have passed by as I committed
the innocent numbers of neighbors to memory and maybe

you were miles away and I, like the woodsman of fairy tales,
threatened all with my bright ax shining with the evil
joy of vengeance and mad hunger to bring harm—heavy

harm—to the coward who did this and if I find you,
my friend, I promise you I will lay the sharp blade deep

into your body until the humid grabbing hands of what must be
death have mercy and take you away from the constant
murderous swinging my mind makes my words make
swinging down on your body and may your children
weep a thousand tears at your small and bewildered grave.

Here the Street Is Narrow

And so when he sees his high-school English teacher
  walk toward him on the sidewalk fifteen years
    after undressing her
  invisibly, nimbly, during hours
of Julius Caesar he says "Hello there, Sweet Tits!"

and she slaps him so hard his glasses fly and break,
  his cheek stings and her hand stings even more
    and he apologizes
  and they stand there together awkward
and neither says a word for about three seconds

and she bends to help him gather the lenses and wire
  but what actually happened no one
    believes—it was sunny
  like a postcard of the Virgin Islands
but late October and the mix of orange and green

leaves on the sugar maples lining the street glowed
  incandescent and she didn't slap him
    and the sugar maples
  glowed incandescent still in the sunny
crystalline blue day of this late October

afternoon and they smiled and talked and he confessed
  charmingly to the high-school crush and how
    often he undressed her
  and she told of feeling a draft often
in that classroom and they went to a hotel room

in the next town over and made love slowly all day
  and that was it—she never called him back
    or returned his letters
  and when she saw him on the sidewalk as
often she did in this small town she said "Hello there,

Cock of the Walk" and laughed and they were friendly
  never talking or saying anything
    but "Hello there, Auburn Hair"
  and "Hello my sweet friend" whispering soft
as they passed on the sidewalk under the sugar maples.

Onlookers with the Burned Body of Jesse Washington, 18-Year-Old African American, Waco, Texas, 1916

His mother at the edge of the crowd, blind with the impossible, standing
mute, agog, gone. And yet the smell of the smoke of her son's body
fills the air around her this May afternoon in Texas. The sun glitters
spectacular as is the custom on May afternoons in Texas and yet

comes through the years as a dull smoky whiteness in the trees here
in the photograph I am tired of looking at. In which there is no woman
whatsoever, especially not the mother of Jesse Washington whose
charred body hangs from a chain in a chestnut tree in Waco Texas

in 1916. Instead, the front row of a crowd of white men all dressed
in suits and ties and fashionable hats stares into the camera. One laughs.
He is the youngest with his sleeves rolled to the elbows. Another
smiles more slyly in the shadow of his hat and appears to be pulling

the slim chain that holds the body of Jesse Washington by the neck
up into the chestnut tree. Though it is probably silver-colored the chain
appears conveniently as the whitest element of the black-and-white.
After it wraps around his neck, it then drapes down the disfigured char

of Jesse Washington's back. Besides these onlookers standing
in the smoke in Texas in May in 1916, three facts are striking.
One is how the legs of Jesse Washington, as the chain pulls him
face-forward into the tree, how his legs bend at the knee and remain

so still burning and smoky where the muscles contract and pull
his feet upward so that if he had the freedom to lie on the ground
and burn he would. Instead it looks as if he is leaping a great
distance, his arms tucked into his chest by the same force that

turns a house to ash. The next fascinating fact of the photograph is
the faded blurry trees in the distance rising up over the crowd.
How filled they are with men. How crowded they are, how intent
they are on looking. As I am. For here in the perch of my second-

floor room of this house in Summit Point West Virginia I have sat
all evening staring at this photograph. I don't know why it interests me.
I know all these men. I was born in May and Texas hasn't changed.
Ask James Byrd Jr. who was so pulled by a truck with a chain.

Most white American men are the same color they were then.
Note the swift progression and the repetition of the true rhymes.
The divisive shift in the tone. If you feel the least bit attacked—
look at that—the final most fascinating fact of the photograph.

Prayer for a Marriage

For Kathleen

When we are old one night and the moon
arcs over the house like an antique
China saucer and the teacup sun

follows somewhere far behind
I hope the stars deepen to a shine
so bright you could read by it

if you liked and the sadnesses
we will have known go away
for awhile—in this hour or two

before sleep—and that we kiss
standing in the kitchen not fighting
gravity so much as embodying

its sweet force, and I hope we kiss
like we do today knowing so much
good is said in this primitive tongue

from the wild first surprising ones
to the lower dizzy ten thousand
infinitely slower ones—and I hope

while we stand there in the kitchen
making tea and kissing, the whistle
of the teapot wakes the neighbors.

For Maurice Sendak

Always in the night
there is a naked boy
flying through the city.
There is a naked boy
floating on his back.
There is a naked boy
hovering over the town
near where you live
and his foot grazes
the high church steeple.
There is another one
upside down sleeping
in the dark branches
of an apple tree. Look
there are hundreds of boys,
hundreds of girls, floating
in the sweet dark of late
late April and soon enough
it will be light everywhere
and the moon will close
its large sensitive eyes.
Its black long lashes
shut when the moon
blinks and the moon
blinks all the time. Now,
quietly, someone floats
through the pine trees
of a yard in Brooklyn
and up around the dark
skyscrapers that tower
over the city and this boy
thinks as the moon sinks
dreaming is like a power
and New York City gets
this sudden and tiny shower.

Ten-Letter Word for a Lucky Man

JimmyTombs you have the best name in the county
         as far as I am concerned and the woman
              I overheard today
         in the way she said your name softly
combining your first and last name into one sound

and she was in the booth behind me at Fran's Place
         and JimmyTombs she said and JimmyTombs
              JimmyTombs, JimmyTombs
         for an hour going on about your
private business and I thought there is no finer

thing ever to happen in a man's life but to have
         a woman fall in love with you
              and for her to sweetly
         tell her friend your name over and over
in a public place and that, JimmyTombs, truly

makes you the luckiest man with the best-sounding
         name in the whole green state of Virginia
              and her friend was quiet
         as your friend spoke and spoons lightly
touched the sides of coffee cups being stirred all over

the restaurant and when the waitress came over
         to clear a dish or ask a question
              of the woman who loves
         JimmyTombs and the friend of the woman
who loves JimmyTombs their conversation stopped

momentarily and I went back to Zippy
         the Pinhead and the crossword puzzle
              in the *Washington Post*
         but it was impossible JimmyTombs
and when my slice of pie came with whipped cream

the waitress carried two other small blue plates
         in her left hand and I listened—
              JimmyTombs—when she said
         "His kiss is like a feather," and we ate
pecan pie—the three of us—quietly, all together.

Luck's Bird over Love's House

For Katie

Sometimes two strangers will meet, fall in love, bear children and die
all in one second and we call this true love and every single moment
after this is a kind of afterlife. And if they part, all their days are hell.

If, on the other hand, they live out the wild dream of that first glance
as if it was love's blueprint and survive the awkward and dangerous
nature of surprise, then they are blessed. And their days are heaven.

And so lovers who were strangers once have a long life after death.
And so a man walks over to a woman and they speak. Or she walks
over to him and they speak. Later they kiss. And the blessings begin.

And the blessings do not stop when you think they should, and this
is the scary part—the sweet feeling of endlessness that is sometimes
accompanied by a feeling of impending doom. The night stars hang

brightly over the neighborhood tonight and a bird with a wingspan
of something so huge it is probably the sky itself flies quietly over
as my father kisses my mother. And that first moment begins again.

Ode to Rosa Parks

In the forests of Alabama where pine trees crowd the air and scrape
        the blue sky raw and heat sifts down a few degrees
where green moss creeps on stones and crawls over the earth,

I will bet all I ever loved that just below the surface here you will find
        the bones of men smashed by roots and the gray rinds
of the skulls of women broken open like sudden storms one at a time

over the brutal southern course of years and you could populate
        three or four medium-sized towns with the bodies lost
in the forests outside Montgomery Alabama and forty-five years of

clear starry nights have passed over these pines since that afternoon
        in December 1955 when you risked the sudden
rage of whites who mobbed up at a moment's notice and the midnight

cruelties of Alabama were practiced so well so often that the smallest
        act of defiance was a matter of life and death and you
did not move to the back of the bus as you were told to and it was

dangerous, always dangerous, to have any courage in the South,
        just to open your mouth, or to breath in and out,
and you did not move to the back of that bus on Cleveland Avenue,

Secretary of the Alabama chapter of the NAACP, Lady Courageous,
        Rosa Parks, sitting in that seat you saved us
the difficult sweet word *free*.

If Every Night You Sleep You Die

A house comes over the mountain singing the blues
      and the ghost of Robert Johnson hollers
         and the ghost of his guitar
    lies in the back of the dark super-charged
blue Cadillac he swerves as he guns to the right

of the house coming over the mountain too fast
      much too fast and a rocket whispers by
         this young man heading back
    to Mississippi and the rocket zooming
wobbles as it goes and Joseph and Mary laugh

while the baby Jesus combs his black pompadour
      with one hand on the controls and maybe
         every time you sleep you die
    and a magnet at the very center
of the universe pulls the house over the mountain

and the mountain follows and the void of space fills
      with objects as lakes and possums arc over
         nothing and join the moon
    and all the paintings of Willem de Kooning
spin ferocious alongside carburetors and refrigerators

from junkyards and the salad fork of a once-great
      restaurant glimmers in the passing light
         of the passing sun gone
    with the death-stained elegant dress
Audrey Hepburn was buried in and a thousand

dogs chasing one cat bark and bark as the jungle
      of Costa Rica floats by like a planet
         and the Garden of Eden
    with Adam and Eve holding on tightly
to the frail bowed end of a young willow tree goes

by your house like a flying saucer and sausage
      on a grill sizzles still heading onward
         and a young woman out
    sweeping the parking lot of a 7-Eleven
laughs as the broom leaps from her small startled hands.

This House

Before the mob of wild roses nodded
and bobbed in the small mid-May
wind this day is made of and before
the oak trees that reach and sprawl
through the upper stories of the air
were ever acorns, this house was built.

One hundred years ago today someone
started the hard good work of digging
with an iron bar. President McKinley
was riding a gray horse slowly down
a quiet twilit street. The gauzy beard
of Walt Whitman, only several years

in the vault of his grave, still gray
still clung to the beautiful ancient
face. And stillness was a tradition
thousands of years old sometimes
interrupted by the long unbearable
agonies of teenagers dying on dark

battlefields in Rome and in Gettysburg.
Stillness on that first day and the man
digging mops his brow with a hand-
stitched kerchief so blue even the sea
pales and seems ghostly in comparison.
He mops his brow and he looks around.

And the house rises up timber by timber,
blue stone by stone and nail by nail
for years and seven arrowheads, one
perfect set of young pterodactyl bones,
two spoons and the diary of John Brown
remain still below the house, unfound.

Three Poems for the Side of a Rocket Going to the Moon on a Saturday Night

1 The Hold

Say something sudden and brilliant—
Boomshakalaka—under the moon,
or dance with your mother soon
in her lonely kitchen or walk
backwards, but do something.
Being's cha-cha is so short.
Breath's bar mitzvah so swift.
Every day and night you and I
zoom like sorrow's antique
rocket towards a certain loss.
Every day all day and every
night we lie in the hold while
what we know grows farther
away and it takes a long time
to say what we mean—hold on,
strangers, hold on and scream.

2 Of Luck

Here is the rain of a night too long.
Here is the dream and the wild song.
Here in these hours nothing happens
by and then moves on and away
while the atoms of the dog glow on
dark red and the window's opening
fills with the architecture of silk
ladders and the spider sways there
gentle in the agony of the fly and I
or some facsimile of white bones
lie in the sleep of midsummer's
falling the rain makes a lullaby
of. Everything trembles, everything
sighs, and everything that you know
and call by name and honor here,
nothing thinks isn't worth the time.

3 Where We Live

Evening comes to surprising ends—
darkness in the bright of things,
noises in quiet stillnesses,
movements under everything.
Ants falling asleep in the colony
dream in the fastness while an owl
cancels the hours of a gentleman
mouse smoking his cigar serene
by the bye and the moon rises
staring at you and the whiz-bang
white jalopy of the afternoon
dies and then before you know it
something on something on
into infinity collapses beside you.
Heaven's dark telescopic blue.
All day today I have loved you.

Summit Point Peace

Sitting on my roof in early May in that time between
the sun's disappearance and the quarter moon's arrival
everything's color deepens and shadows sprig up
like new shoots of the oncoming darkness and I see

the wheelbarrow below me and the mucky shovel there
resting in it and the chicken coop collapsing
second by second in its slow love for the ground
and decay takes the rabbit in the yard that died

of natural causes and if you think the very beginnings
of a hornet's nest hanging on the eaves just behind
my ear threaten the twilight's sense of security—no.
One hornet grips the tiny two-comb masterpiece of

paper and saliva and this house is certainly more
its than mine and all the millions of hornets flying
with their delicate legs dangling a little all over
the world know they have dominion and cruise

in their high creaturely way and the walnut tree
a little to the east of my sleeping cat finally works
a few leaves onto its dark branches and every
morning the sparrows applaud in a jumpy excited

windblown way among the thickening leaves and if
you have a cell-phone sitting in some kind of silly
leather holster attached to your hip then you are already
more important than me and most of our friends

who sometimes gather here for dinner on the back porch
and drink bourbon and eat pasta and tell stories
while someone at the far end of Summit Point grows
sleepy and lies down and a fox barks in the orchard.